to know you

to know you

POEMS IN CELEBRATION OF REVELATION

ALLYN BENEDICT

iUniverse, Inc.
Bloomington

to know you
Poems in Celebration of Revelation

iUniverse books may be ordered through booksellers or by contacting:

iUniverse
1663 Liberty Drive
Bloomington, IN 47403
www.iuniverse.com
1-800-Authors (1-800-288-4677)

ISBN: 978-1-4697-8811-1 (sc)
ISBN: 978-1-4697-8812-8 (ebk)

Printed in the United States of America

iUniverse rev. date: 03/07/2012

Contents

Revelation in Life By Faith 29

A word about a beginning

Poetry began, for me, as a gift given by my friend, Michael Harper: brother; poet; servant friend of God. I dedicate this book to him.

I had had a wonderful visit with Michael and his wife, Jane, in their home in Tumbridge Wells, England. At the time, Michael was head of medicine and Chief Executive of Burrswood, a Christian Hospital and healing center, there among the rolling hills—the green, green, sheep studded hills—of Kent. We had walked those hills, sharing our minds and our hearts. In the evenings he had opened his poetry notebooks and translated the prescriptive squiggles dashed there over the course of some years; vibrant, moving (laughter waiting in the wings but not for long), delivered by a gifted reader—the spontaneous outpourings of a creative and agile mind, yoked with a discerning heart. Add a finger or two of fine single malt whisky. A fire in the hearth. Fellowship in height and depth, spiced with a shared, honed appreciation of the ridiculous. Always under the threat of an outbreak of joy: we were, after and under all, in our Father's house and about his business. Brothers.

As I left for Heathrow and my return flight, Michael handed me an envelope with contents to be read on the plane. As soon as we lifted off, I opened the gift. It was a poem celebrating the time we had just had together. A lovely, strong poem.

A response welled up: a poem in return (*"Friendship's Loss"*). Michael had, by the grace of God, I believe, primed a pump in me. I began to draw from a familiar creative well. I had drawn music from that well in my former life as a composer and I have come to understand that poetry is just another way that music escapes me. One more manifestation of the mystery of creative life in the One who is Life.

Feel free to sing along.

Allyn Benedict
Bedford, Virginia
November, 2011

REVELATION IN CREATION

"For since the creation of the world God's invisible qualities . . . have been clearly seen, being understood from what has been made."

[Romans 1:20]

If I lived here long

If I lived here long
Would I begin to hear
The oak and hemlock pray,
Or stone begin to heave
And rise with bolder voice
To praise a rock that's higher?

Perhaps it's not so strange:
Rough stone, shaped and purely thankful now—
God's found treasure in this field;
Hemlock stirred to windward worship by the one
Who breathed out sparrow, seal and star;
Who spoke this stone and singing oak;
Who whispered and I was.

Because his breath is life and sweet
My limbs too are raised.
And earth-bound though I am
I'm heaved up into praise of him,
who is my rock—
Whose Spirit birthed and stirred
This current breath of praise that's mine.
But never mine alone.

The gift of an evening dawn

Does any wild wood wonder search
or move the heart more deeply
than a dappled beech at six;
parting gift from a sun
turning toward another dawn?

Unless it be one hyper-leaning birch,
which in the wake of some past wind
has toppled over into trust
and now seems gladly lost
in this old hemlock's evergreen embrace.

Now at vaguely eight,
when sharp leaves dull in dimming light,
I yield these brimming,
less discriminating eyes to keener sight,
when the gift of an evening dawn
breaks dappled in the depths of me.
And trust can breathe,
and I have leave to lean again.

there are buds

there are buds
sprays of
sunset garlands of
buds aloft
splay fingered tops of
twig-tip jewels of
greening bud-burst trees

final glory seen today
bar one faraway winger
pattern perfect
on a perfect evening sky
above these land-spring trees
April supple with a sap-hope
much like mine surging up
from soiled root to buds
sprays of
dusk riots of

October trees

October trees
have revelation leaves
apocalyptic maples utter
startled flaming joy
unimaginable brightness of birch lilt
lyric motives

leading hill-home brethren into
scores of yellow songs of yielding
russet valleys sing content though filled
with knowledge of the deep
and final falling notes

of their richly seasoned song
all reflections of the One who sings
of his willingness to live all flaming Love
descending down

and down and sinking dark alone
(for joy of our glad rising day)
to lightless depths where we

who knew no yielding song or startled joy
or full throat tree or revelation leaf

were found.

the ways of winter

I can see the ways of winter
melting out of fashion
spring's the passing fevered passion
flickering fires are out
in this higher innovative sun

today's arctic intimation's
robbed of power by a tropic hope
one tiny song-bird
lifts this weather weight
a back yard glacier
heaved up by a flower

not that snow's condemned
for being crystalline
or wind
for complicity with cold
only that a winter's lengthy grip
has warmed a new affection

a friend departs who stayed too long
this deep sigh is not relief alone
there's loss in turns
from one love to another

so warm by here

from outside dark
a sound
a scraping
gravelly grating
an iron scritch
listen
listen
lift a little off the pillow
hear

a huge heavy
shabby orange block of a
high throned bull of a plow truck
heaves up snow

a merciless concave mass
of sharp wedge steel
battles tiny flakes
(every one a wonder)

sure a futile barren tilling
so this screeching
so this beastie wailing
this howling so

surely not
listen new
this is summer
hearing rushes in
from a roadway to my rib:
it's just my dear old girl
snoring comfy snug
warm
so warm by here

very early in the day
In Idaho

very early in the day
a brightening in the east
quickly thinning cloud
dawn rises blue
offers this ovation
and I am glad
though I was glad for the rain
pleased for alpine flowers and trees
and for the sake of music in the night
(a music like no other)
for myriad timbres
the sounds of showers
soft on timbers
paradiddles patter windows
pitter splatting stones and tile
sharp clips slapping cedar shingles
tip tap aspen quivering
music with unknown
yet perfect form
primal rhythmic counterpoint
searching out my blood
all of which was good
and now this blue applause

Last moments of a life

last moments of a life can now be seen
on the glass of a sliding door
fixed there living and livid
where I caused him to be
a hunter hornet (huge by the scale
of his captors) writhes awhile
caught in the intrigue of a web

I watch impressed with spiders again
this one stuns and wraps routinely
while by her side a replica
a tiny apprentice of her dance
scurries in and out again
touches tomorrow's dinner then retreats
a brave arachnid counting coup

apart from my design
I see there's fresh provision
better for all concerned I think
even for the doomed
than the crushing blow intended
when I swung some tightly rolled
if long outdated news

news of scores from a long forgotten night
winners and losers in the games of spring
and of a small plane lost in fog
whose pilot with his fishing friend
praying to come home again
ended in the window of a living room
both unharmed and yet undone

the story of a couple lost at sea
who planned to circumnavigate
before the dread uncertainties of Y2K
news of a new heart none too soon
for a teen who now must be a man
who long ago twisted gripped by fear
but rescued went his way again

I know the wind that splits an oak

I know the wind that splits an oak
and raises up a roof with ease
and wailing drives the clipper ship
presses down its sails
dunks its rails in the wind heaved sea

I know another wind today
its skittering fingertips
whisking briskly
feather stroke airs barely ruffling
the calm complexion of a pond

this is shear raw power too
not a kind to raise the roof
not the power to rile the sea
but a weary heart is lifted up
an anxious world is stilled

I heard him calling
on our anniversary

I heard him calling
in the dark
jeh-wee jeh-wee
he said
jeh-wee jeh-wee
he meant
he's a bird
and in his heart
he sings of many things
of feline stealth
of thorny twigs
and seedy wealth
but to my ear
it always sounds the same

then with the sun
came shocking
new song
jeh-wee jeh-wee
jeh-wee jeh-wee
jeh-wee this
he sang
this he meant
this it seemed to me was
blatant novelty
odd and nervy
for an ordinary day
symptom of a mind
unmoored no less

full throated yes
but a verbose bird
a bird perched
on the edge of hysteria
a bird unglued
stirs my heart
and I thought
what's in this for you
birdie was it simply true
that jeh-wee jeh-wee
didn't seem enough
to sing this morning's glory
was it beauty
drove you south

then it dawned on me
this was a she and not
a he and he
was late and his
own counter call
was loudly absent here
and as the hawk of fear
began to wheel
she waxed prolix
for tender reason's sake
when no familiar song
jeh-wee jeh-wee could free
or serve to sound
her anxious heart

then I heard his answer
in the broken dawn
jeh-wee jeh-wee
he sang
jeh-wee jeh-wee
he meant and more
but could not find a way
to sing of his long flight
or his own anxious cry
but now at last this finding
now this meeting
two now sounding this
one song
one this thrilling day

Advent earthquake

I heard from the crèche
the tinkle sound of falling
as I played the baby grand
as I strode the heights
and wept the depths
of utterly unseasonable Schumann

later I discovered
the not-yet-heralding angel
shaken by a forte had fallen
face first from safe heights
into a far from stable manger
(not yet with child)
in starlit balsa Bethlehem
on quaking polished ebony earth
(even the ceramic folded cudding cow
and all the sheep were moved)
while nearby
a shepherd come early
like his flock overcome
canted by earth-shifting exultation
had turned
was leaning
reclining face first
weeping
on the bosom of his friend
with prophetic joy

I am discipled
"Not one of them will fall . . ." Matthew 10:29

I am discipled
I am wounded
by a soaring wood flute
a thrush tuned to wonder
ecstatic trilling
breaks my heart

from a great height
her florid cry arching
like woodwind lightning
strikes me twice and
I am busted
I am opened

by her song and by
her silence schooled
by silence too
I'm tutored
in the interval of pauses
as she listens

sings then listens
and I learn
as I am shattered
by simplicity
to know she simply is
and just as simply

she will one day be
all silence without pause
but I remember that
the Father knows his own
sweet woodwind singer

so her silence will be heard

winter dawn

early cumulous caught fire
underbellies lit by a matchless sun
not yet seen
but heard in riot rose-glow
conflagration cloud sopping spilt flame
a tolling depth ignited in the heights

Cardinal

chest puffed
crest head high
he starts a downward
sweetly liquid whistle
then rapid throat throbs
tapping nineteen to the bar

he sounds those ancient taps
on ancient cardinal doors
within her breast
will they open will-she nil-she
will she simply flit to him
servant of a primal sound

or will she willing choose
perhaps the rhythm of another
one whose liquid crimson song
echoes now more sweetly
in the ancient cardinal chambers
of her heart

early reflections

being in the heavens suspended
prone
reflecting
planets at my back
facing prospects of a pond
I see unsettled stars
a mutable sky
am moved
by current-scattered pedals
of a fragile lunar flower
and my flowing rippled form

being on the pond alone
buoyed by an undulating dawn
I see the fading stars
see faintly silhouetted leaves
of dimly back-lit trees
and myself
in heaven high suspension
in rapt reflection
stirred
by a pond-sown
sliver moon

I pass myself
in the looking glass

Heading to the loft for sleep
I pass myself.
How long have I been waiting
to be seen there as I am?
Passing through this rough-cut
hemlock paneled, cabin room:
old man walking under trees.

With rest these steep, few steps away,
I see myself and know
I'm coming to the brink:
the arch of a new day—
a fine first day of a new season.
A season of promise.
A promise first received,
then a promise made.

I will not pass you by.
I will go up.
I will receive your rest
and your new day.
I will not fail to climb the trees
and wonder at the stars.

ALLYN BENEDICT

The canceller of heights
Helmsdale, Scotland

Heavy cloud drifting up the glen
carries and delivers rain;
cancels heights by being there;
hazes all the rest,
except this slender swatch
of fenced in flowers.
Turned back now from veiled distance,
my sight is narrowed:
brought to bear on nearby columbine,
on this lucid, yielding tree,
on earlier, inner, shortened sight—
my non-transparency.

To me my heart became obscure,
clouded by the storm I was today.
But after the common struggle;
after turning in the light;
after squinting in the temple,
I've begun in faith to see
(through my lashes and my dark)
his side, and, cruelly carpentered,
the strong, surrendered hands
that still the storm,
unveil the upland Kite,
and cancel out the canceller of heights.

a new sun

a new sun blossoms in this pear tree
on the still dark featureless bark of its trunk
on every limb and twig and bud
and all along an early robin's breast
Easterly gilding on the sunward edge

There is a stillness now

there is a stillness now
come with the late day sun
and with stillness comes a word
not a word from the radiant tops of nearby trees
or the luminous spine of a distant ridge
not from a current drifter
a hunter hawk who rides in the glowing
his cold eye down

this word is the truth of a beauty
not spoken in the flung-silver song of a thrush
not by a Barred owl octaves down
in the hollow-huff-whos of his horn call
it sounds with the sun's last light
but is not the loveliness of that light
it is the word in an evening stillness
who whispers a Sabbath rest

a first snow

a first snow
a cold north wind
I welcomed
and their companion warmth
hearth home
a flame

love of cold comes in context
liberty to love this deadly beauty
comes with a door in easy distance
comes with prospect of a certain journey
from blizzard to blaze

and if there is no fire
no hope of a threshold
no certain hearth
where's the way in from fear
where's the way
when warmth is not secure
where's the way if context is lost
and winter stalks alone
grips then shoves a cicle blade
thrusts my heart solid in a second

I never could be calm
not free in cold
apart from known retreat
could not survive this enemy
with no way home
and frozen eyes that see no fire
see no kin
no way out
no way in

Virginia in between
a September song of trees and trains

this morning is not hot
neither is it cold
a lukewarm day idles near
fills my eye and I begin to see
sidles up and whispers in my ear
and I begin to hear

a faintly whistling rustle
the brittle whispered song
of drying leaves less darkly green
but not yet glorified
the throaty woodwind song
of summer ambling south again

I hear a steely basso rumble
out beyond these subtle trees
a distant voice of raucous warning
chants its burden down a track
chides a searing August spent
cautions heightening autumn to relent

Cornwall wind
Gribbin Head, Cornwall, England

Cornwall wind braces me, salt fresh,
whipping sharp from the sea,
quick and straight across this bluff—
a towering bluff and this path: exaltation high!
But far too edge-close for inside-ease,
what with that other (that imagined) wind
streaming out to sea with me in it,
fancifully over the shale-flake lip and gone.
Am I prepared for such a sudden shift?
If this headland wind comes hard around,
can I avoid a verge that's shearly madness, nothing more?
Will I know the terror of a flailing mind
and screams from above and rock at last?

Down below and down-a-down the coast ahead,
rocks like bared, blackened, broken teeth;
Cornwall teeth pounded, pounded with no mercy.
Teeth in ancient, comber stricken, Gribbin mouths
spewing white-blood, lace-spit spray,
while to my right and higher up,
whiskered, sagging, sweet, unimaginative cows
pay no mind to smash-mouth seas
or the glory ruination of waves;
know nothing of a quickened pulse out beyond their hedge.

And yet I find I'm filled and glad, not least for this unease.
Glad to pick each step, as I do, so near the edge.
Glad of a wind that moves, as it does, as it wills with me.

REVELATION IN LIFE BY FAITH

"What is more, I consider everything a loss compared to the surpassing greatness of knowing Christ Jesus my Lord . . ."

[Philippians 3:8]

to know you

to know you in this moment

Lord is to love you
with my yes this time

faith is what I do in light of you

the rest darkness no matter
these bright words

I'll live my yes

in making this time yours
newly your creation

my moment's dim yes

caught in the radiance of yours
(whose I am

or there's no light

my moments yours or my life
remains my own)

let your desire burst
and from divine debris in me

coalesce new heart stars

shape bright worlds
in orbits of your will

a galaxy of days

that give
you

glory

Friendship's Loss

O Lord,
You know:
It's no single thing alone I've lost
In knowing this new friend.

Isolation's lost, for one.
Lost the longing for meeting.
Lost the ache to be received.

Dark is lost come this warm, bright ray,
Like an early ray of that Last Day:
That dawn of loss and light
When dark worlds are shut tight
And heaven's open for highest meeting.
When faith is lost for sight of you.
When partial things fall away—
Gladly lost in glory!

Lost the loss of You.
Lost this mortal coil.
Lost this wound that will not heal.

But this warm, bright ray's good 'til Sonrise!
So I thank you, Father, for this surprise.
For this friend.
This loss.

Will your holy hill
Repentance

Will your holy hill rise from humbled sands
of my desert heart;
your heights from the low place
where I have come to mourn and turn?

My broken heart is what I give to you;
it is your handhold here in me.
Get a grip.
Lift me
by this purchase I provide.

Jesus, find and seize me grieving
with those steady hands of yours,
grown so strong with planing;
roughed and strong from knowing adz and saw;
stronger than death from knowing nails
that fix my sin to grace.

Search relentless Lord.
Reach deep in me,
your wounding friend, and
mark your signs in my heart sand.
Then in every hour ascend in me
to heights of you
by paths that I will follow.

sun can't heat the place

warming summer sun can't heat
the place where cold has come
where a high and lively word
came low and into silence
a moving part stilled
like a drawn breath held

come breathe in me
you breath of me my joy
Holy Spirit thaw me
with a roaring lick of flame
and I will move again
and stutter in your heat
glory-faced with morning
in the updraft of your word

convalescent visions
patient vision 1

he suggests the latter Pavarotti
in the haystack sense,
but his air
(a burden too great to bear alone)
was a groan all night

we in the ward are fed his moans
        his groans
        his alarm
every species of well manured complaint
pruned to a forced riot of thorns among contemptible
roses
        every single one the same
        never mind the name
that clamber up and top his neighbors' walls
all dusk long
all night long
all bleeding dawn
        never mind the day

He preaches his question
        in a memorable feat of amnesia
"Why?" he asks,
        thinking he's plumbed the depths—
        that he's spit his question
        in God's eye for us all.
"'Why?'" the ward replies.
"we'll tell you why
        never mind your moans
        never mind your night songs
        or your night soil flowers:
you've plumbed nothing.

it's all that pie, Pavarotti."

(convalescent visions)
nurse vision

I see her
this starched student
a dark-eyed daughter
come like a butterfly
drawn to sweet service
pert cool-hand apple
of my recent opened eye

twenty three and brave
she softly lifts her questions
not yet routine
about my body's functions
"I have to ask", she says
looking at her shoes

later she leans
looking closely at a vein
slides the needle in
  searching
  sowing pain
withdraws
exhales
  searches once again
  at last she finds
  "I'm . . . sorry" she says
"Why?" I say searching
"You've done what you must"
"I hate to hurt
I'm sorry to cause you pain".
  she retains the tears
  that threaten her cheek

"I know
but there are times
when in order to love
we must cause pain
so thank you"

I do not say "for loving me"
yet she reaches to receive
gathers this gift
          these words not spoken
with two dark eyes
in one quick upward glance

(convalescent visions)
patient vision 2

Pavarotti has a wife
she visits one whole afternoon
a woman reserved
        nearly frumpy
        but not
a woman patient
with a faint water-color wash
of long suffering
she's cared for him alone
much as he is
for years
now he moans alarm
        she murmurs
he sleeps
        she reads
he recounts
        she encourages

they share a subtle something like a smile

he sleeps
        she sows

at last she prepares to leave
        I feel with her what I take to be relief
as she gathers herself and rounds the bed
one more duty to perform I think
I see a peck coming
a cool pucker
a time-card punch
her shift at an end
and sure enough she rounds the bed
heading for his brow
sure enough she puckers up
her lips come down

but they do not lift
they linger softly
much longer than required
her ring hand resting gently
on the acre of his chest
her lips shift a little to the side
   a second delicate planting
then begin to travel
warm kisses
not hen pecking
a love journey to loved sites
moving warm to his cheek
then to his brow
and round and tender round
the best part of a minute
of such sweetness
more than enough
to break my heart

the beloved makes no response
does not look as she leaves
I know the reason
it's his heart condition
his heart's been taken
   in hands yielded
his heart blessed
his heart broken

he goes with her
his treasured heart
in the heart of his treasure

here I go again

here I go again
boasting of defeat
prematurely counting heaven's chickens
but you drive me to it Jesus
your progress on my battle front
corners me in hope
in the first flush of your victories over me
I begin to swagger strut and bluster
that my "old man's" cause is lost
and rushing on I trumpet my sin's ruin
I come running toward your throne in me
proudly waving my surrender
but you've heard the rebel whisper in my heart
trumpet tunes or not
and you know my will to wander's
not as flagging as it seems
yet here I've run and here your arms
and here I go again
from the shelter of your holding bragging
lord you're occupying all the high ground
in my heart
all rebellion's famished in this city under siege
see a withered idol
there a starving lust
I swear I've lost the war to win my way
and so I go on talking like a fool

with your light bright in my eyes
your shackles on my heart
your word subduing holdouts
in the hideouts of my mind
your relentless new creating
cut the legs of prudent caution
out from under me
so down I went and here I am
and here I go again
boasting of defeat
but you drive me to it Jesus
yes you do
you know you do

Father I will run

Father I will run
free in harvest fields

the saddle off
the reins and bit removed

free and bound by you
free in your desire

now become the blood in me
now my heart bread
now my soul delight

speak of doors

speak of doors where doers
of the Word walk willing
of grain now threshed
beyond the threshold

of heart's high stepping
into harvest fields
words of seeding Word
of Spirit's wind winnowing

speak of sharp decision sword
thrust to joint and marrow
of Peace who brings division
(meet with joy this cleaving

welcome threshing power past
the threshold of this choosing)
and of harvest in a heart
that wills one thing

life you're here

life you're here
your horizon seen
a going out gift
hope with a voice
new song risen for the road

purifying water
floods the bitter
your spring rains
drench me once again
sweetness Lord and further in

who could tire
of such mornings
of your birthings
of unchanging love
for living new again

Joy in a high heart
Helmsdale, Scotland

Joy in a high heart lift up now.
Trickling, life-giving waters merge.
Flood the gate and sink the well.
Over run my river verge.

I stand on the side of a stony hill
and see in the distance a sheltering bay;
but I've not come for safety or breakwater calm,
I climb for strength that's known within;
for alien calm in the teeth of a wind;
for peace on an open, heaving sea.

Joy come on breakers—heave me high.
Life-flooded-heart song, slip my lips!
Pour out freely—fill the dell.
Spill like a rill from my fingertips!

A sunset is as a sunrise is,
albeit they're opposite ends of a day.
And the road that will narrow and draw to a close
may seem to look and walk the same
as the road that rises, opening out
through an arch, to a bright new way.

Joy run the roadway opening now!
Leap from the top of my heart's desire!
Praise with the stones from the peak of me!
Dance up the narrow way like fire!

Not yet my Eastertide

Joy! Joy, they sing,
for his rising.
Joy dear friends
with this day's dawn.
After all his pain,
thorn's oppression gone.
So Joy!
Joy to the heart!
But I have none.

Hope! Hope, they say.
From his flesh
(at the base of a stony slope)
a living-hope spring
of his blood.
And we are one.
So Hope!
Hope in the heart!
But I have none.

Light! Light from the tomb,
they sing.
Light from light,
with this good new day.
After darkness on a bare death tree,
light-soaked healing leaves.
It is done!
Light for the heart!
But I have none.

Those still on a cross
have no joy,
but a spear to the heart
and loss.
She had John's
and he her broken heart.
But I am stripped of all
except abandonment.

Those still on a cross
have no hope,
for hopelessness that's seen
is no hope at all.
I thirst here in the dark.
No light for the heart has come
to penetrate this stone.
My kingdom for a friend.
But I have none.

like preaching which is leaping

life's at times
like preaching which is leaping
I search for a start before I see a finish
I release a sound before I have a word
I begin a word before I know the next
then one phrase
(or say one day)
leaps like a diver
springs to heights then
swoops down filled with grace
toward the hope of a cool deep stream
I know abounding freedom in the flowing of His wind
until I see that I am well beyond where water could
have been
and taken in the iron fist of fear
(gripped for a word or for one phrase
or for a month or two)
I begin to falter faithlessly
until I feel His joy again
His deep delight in taking hold of me
with the strong so gentle hands of His heart
and He lifts me up
and softly sets me down
delivered to a high and open place
a strong rock of His love where I am satisfied
filled again with trust for the living of a life
like preaching which is leaping

trust for us

trust for us
when needed most
as in the face of fear

is like compassion
intruding on contempt

more like hope
imposing on despair

most like hunger
penetrating stone

I look to the hills

Remembering my father who took his life

I look to the hills,
I look to the sea,
As my life runs out like a river.

The valley is sweet,
The clouds low and scudding.
My life's running down like a river.

My father long gone,
My father not known,
You took back your gift,
And I cannot live mine for the both of us.

Your loss was your loss
And your loss my own.
(Was your own sorrow deep,
O my Lord? Did you weep for the both of us?)

Your days were so short,
While mine have grown long.
But all days run out
To the sea; they run down to the Giver.

I look to the sea,
I look to the hills,
As my life flows up like no river.

The valley is sweet,
The clouds high and scudding;
My life's flowing out for the Giver!

The burden of the highlands
Helmsdale, Scotland

Green is not green;
red is not red ;
a river not a river here.

Green is the land;
red is the road;
the river is a parable.

The land goes from bright chartreuse of white dotted
pastures
to emerald and olive depths of richness on the heights.
The road is a narrow winding thread—
the warp of an ancient highland tartan.

The parable is as a parable does:
it points to power ruling in the heart.

Land—tartan—parable: all speak of faith's descent

From light filled trust and a Word-hued heart,
to pride become a toxin, seeping into soil
and sweet green pastures poisoned with contempt.

From the clothing of the righteousness of Christ,
to the fabric of honor torn as truth is torn from love
and the clothing of revenge that covers grief.

From hearts that see God's glory in the witness of the
moors,
to the harboring of the violence of a godless wind
and bondage to the addicting power of freedom's
counterfeit.

But the parable of the Lord has come,
is coming and will come.
It will not change.

Its eternal seed is being sown in tears.
It speaks of selling all sins' idols and the purchase of a
pearl.
It tells of two lost highland sons and power for both to
enter in.

And Jesus holds the weeping orphans
of indifference and habituated hate,
and shares his heart with women
on their bitter, long ancestral roads of loss.

The Shepherd brings a clearance
of all violence in the glen.
With freedom he clothes
the wounded heart that bows.
On the face and hands that lift to him
he breathes the anointing of his peace.

Over the highlands, the fouling reign will pass away.
The rainbow of the Father's promised life is arched:
his love is seen in the vaulted spectrum of his
faithfulness.
He prepares the way of blessing in the deep red of his
love.

Daily he searches the horizon for his sons;
goes out for precious daughters
from rock shore to high moor.
In and through his body he'll complete the work begun;
the Lord will hunt and woo

Until the river is his power,
red becomes his robe,
and all the green his home.

I bend my knee
Joshua 3:14-4:7

I bend my knee
where the river was
gather smooth stones
with desert rough hands
shoulder each to an open
upland windblown place

there I see them altar shaped
still river wet with memory
of mercy's power bent to me

may this outward altar signify
and be my scattered will
gathered by his hand
my nomadic heart lifted up
and shouldered back again
to a higher altar inward

that holy truest worship site
which the Spirit makes of me
and no world wind can shift

beyond my hope

Jesus I can't hope
to hope to heights of you
unless you hope in me
you're beyond my faith
unless you put your trust in me

you're too high for my thought
unless you speak your mind
unless I'm humbled by your truth
unless you set me free to yield
and lift my thought to you

you're beyond my hope to reach
in the distance of my numbered days
by the span of my obedience
or the arch of my desire
unless you make your way in me

# of Jesus two small requests

(after hearing of a certain "seed your ministry" movement which sounded like a 2 Corinthians 9 based acquisition strategy: donate to other people's ministry so that God will increase your "seed" and prosper your ministry . . . probably an inaccurate and/or incomplete description. But no matter . . .)

first request

a small request from your servant Lord
I know I've preached all day
about you dying there shattered
for the sake of your Father's enemies
but would you rise up now
would you do some pounding with your fist
or flash briefly with wild John's forecast fire
if not an ax

if and as you love me Lord
demonstrate it not with thorns
but with an old-school crowning
no matter what it takes
even if it means you condescend
and enter this ruin again
this time your Father's fist made flesh—
our "just deserts" incarnate—
would you rise up (over the one
who cannot be named)
and wallop all mightily down
Lord with the strength of stars
with the weight of a blow descending
with such a universe of force as would crater
the whole of hell itself

as you can see Lord
I've in mind nothing subtle
so lay aside your Father's justly famed relenting
make a fist
(make it a double)
wield your persuader Lord if you love me
or do it for your sake because I love you
because it's in your own best interest
because I'm watching out for you
(and if I don't who will)

Lord I see you want a word with me
but would you practice your celebrated patience
I can't take a breath quite yet
cold contempt's a knot
in my gut
bile gathers solid in my fist
but a fist too weak for my cause or yours
so this small request again:
when your might descends
don't spread your power thin
no comprehensive blow
we need to focus now
ordnance only Lord
I'll aim
you strike
of course we'll sound a warning you and I
too short before the blow for him to move
just long enough for me to step aside
just time for him to know it's you
that nullifying force descending fast
(and just for him)
revealed as no unthinkable mistake
but as carefully conceived
arriving with unthinkable intent
delivered by your sovereign hand clenched
that was opened once wide and hammered
for his sake

give him time to hear again
the words he's flung
under the banner of your name
words I've seen your Spirit fling away
do it for the worshipped heights of your great name
(and for your cross as well)
for the name he's dragged through the hell
of a thorn-strewn gospelette:
"the almighty
(the indulgent uncle—
his will reconciled to your 'old man')
waits with bated breath
for your success
so leverage your offering high my friend
convert God's promise into cash
'seed your ministry'
and leave some cash with me

though there are others
if I had my druthers you'd
leave a stack with me

maybe I'm guessing
but I call it blessing
so seed your money with me

all that now matters
though Christ be in tatters
is eau de biblical strategy"
(my French is rusty Lord
but in any tongue
we're talking toilet water
with a faint biblical scent)

give him the gift of just enough time
as your power descends
to hear it all again
final echo of his course correction
of the Father's direction in you
his attempted re-placement
of your wide open hands

for it was not a nail you were to grip
you were supposed to embrace a lie:
"go quick! give more of your love away
that this cup may pass you by"

second request

are you done?
    Ok yes
    thank you Lord
    I'll take a breath
yes
breathe in
breathe out
a nice deep breath
feel better?
    no
    well maybe a little
    I am breathing
    I'm calmer
I know
    the knot's not so knotted
I know
    my fist is opening
I know
    I know you know
I know
    I know you know I know
    I know you know I know you . . .
I love you
    I know

and I love him
I love the one you cannot name
    I know
    I do know

Jesus . . . what happened?
you lost your way
you climbed up high for a while
and did what you condemn
oxygen is thin up there: you forgot that I . . .
are you listening
yes
I'm the judge
I know
I know you know

you know it's good that you stopped
that you are breathing
that you see
but I don't Lord
I don't see how you work
with servants like us
that's good
what's good?
the "us"
yes
I know Lord

I know it's good that my hand is open again
I'm looking up again
seeing again
I'm back at your feet
face it Lord
me on the throne is not good
yes

can you lift me up Lord?
can you take my hand?
well . . . my hand's all balled up in a fist here. I don't
think I can, uh . . . that I can get the, uh, get the fingers
to . . . .
you're funny Lord

you're funny too . . .
when you're looking up

when I'm looking up . . . and breathing
when I'm seeing . . .
then I know
I know I want your hand open for me
it is
and so I want it open for what's-his-name
it is
that's good.

but use it to whack him open handed
upside the head about the "seed your ministry" dung
and don't hold back . . .
would you Lord?

breathe beloved
my beloved, open hand;
my open, harvest-field hand
know I am God
I know
know you're not me
you're mine
Yes Lord
that's what I know best when I'm looking up

Take my hand.
    I will . . .
    I am

there's one more thing to know
    yes Lord

for love I'll move him in truth
with my open hand
if he will be moved by love
and open to the truth of me
    that's good Lord

you too
I'll move you too
    I know

    one more thing Jesus
    another small request:
yes

    me first
    for his sake
    start with me

I Will . . .

I AM

I'll ride

I'll ride a roller coaster if I can.
No time for vain ambition at the top;
no stultifying level time
to measure where I've come against a hope or fear;
no time to plot or dull, grow slack or stale.

And in the pits, no temptation to despair of soaring up;
no thought of slogging on for slogging's sake;
just this rushing swoop and gulp—
the valley gone almost before it's here—
and then this lift again,
this rising up with two arms wide,
and facing in to summit wind, this cry aloud:

sovereign hands have held
the heights and depths where I have been,
and when I stand, it's sovereign love who holds me in!

beyond our minding

while the Father's life
breaks like waves
on outward shores
the roaring of his sea change sounds
in caverns never seen

we're held in faith for life
known and loved
beyond our minding
raised up higher
than a conscious hope

while loving him without
we know and love within
our thankful yes maturing
even when our lips are stilled
or mind gone wondering

there companionship is found
with one whose eyes speak paradise
whose joy transforms the core of us
who suffers with us on our cross
who is the pioneer of loss

Our life in your eyes
together with our grandson

Suddenly I see
our life in your eyes.
Tonight in a few quiet moments
I see the passage there
and the promise and even
(because suddenly I see
from the peak of a gift)
the purpose.
In a streaming clarity I know
we see the golden fruit as one.
I see we know as one the joy of those
who love another's eyes.

My spirit's on a lucid height;
my deepest string
plucked with gale force tenderness.
I know a vibrant peace
and hear the full harmonic spectrum
of our common sigh;
a fundamental unison—
an infant gift
found there in the double cream velvet
of our grown girl's own sweet baby's nape;
there in the crook above his collar bone
of my bone;
there inhaled in sweet-sour flesh
of my flesh.
North his corn silk hair.
West your welling eyes,
which I love,
and where suddenly I see
from a sounding gift of height.

I sit for you
a grandfather's tale

you bright mysterious bud
not so far away
being no great gulf between old me
and freshly you that can't be spanned
with not quite guileless smiles
with words not in the air
that say I see you there
that say I see you see me here
you know I know you know
that I am yours
my eyes unveiled

earlier I saw
the crayon smile you draw
on every creature of your hand
you said it was my own
Grampi's ear to ear
saw my porthole eyes
(wide in view of sea change)
both my wind-blown sailor-trouser legs
disconnected circle feet
finger sticks on arms with attitude
a masterpiece of hair

later I began to see
you only said it's me because
you saw my Hope filled eye
you gave your child my name
just to give an aging mystery joy
you drew us just the same
and so we are
and not so very far apart
these sixty years no more
and a hall and a door

reading as I sit for you
I hear you snuffle in your bed
hear your muffled intermittent wail
walk the hall to listen at the door
wonder as I enter is this trouble or a ploy
sense there's been some heavy weather here
the air is charged
and you electric in your lair
tremulous peeking troubled out
with sweat-soaked hair
its plastered strands awry
and there between two fingers
one wild eye

all my caring questions die alone
you've become a mute
and I no longer known

with doors between us closed
reading once again
I sit for you

'til comes your sequel squall
'til comes your desperate turn
seems the old can't know without a word
seems the mute's obliged to speak
if she's to have the one who stills the storm
so I'm known and drawn again
see a second portrait by your hand:
before I sit I shall return
walking on the water

with your cat

here's a howdy do
on the completion of a "final" draft

here's a howdy do
this book's done
and if done
simply meant an end
surely this is one
one thing done
but simply it is not
this done is more
is just begun
this done's a diving board
or as I see it now
a door
not a door
where I've come in for good
though good it is this door
goes out
and who I ask
who could stay this side
the done side of a door
I could but I will not
I will go out
as I have always done
out one by one
until I'm well
and truly done
and seemingly go out
no more
which is of course
another door

Jesus you sang
"And when they had sung a hymn they went out to the Mount of Olives"

Matt. 26:30

Jesus you sang
just as we have
through the ages
round the fire
in the hall
you sang too
you the form
of the word of us
I see your eyes
you the apple of his eye
lit face lifted up
shaped notes streaming
heart to heart

as in your last lamb day
when your final song
came coda to silence
not this praise
not with friends
but jagged lovelorn song
released alone
not this resonate antiphony
but pierced and piercing melody
torn from your torn heart
there on Calvary
shaped by agony
cried aloud in victory

this local hill

I used to think my stride
was three miles long
and both feet wide
the way of shorter guarded steps
seemed lame
a threat to hobble hope
and plod a flaming vision out
what use had mincing steps
to a pilgrim tramping macroscapes
halting gaits lead to forests
lost for trees
glories of expanse
unseen for scrabbling in a ditch
megavital metaphoric cascade falls
parsed to a torpid puddle

miles on, essences remain
now as then my heart is drawn
to tramp deep down to the 3 mile core
of the way of love
though I limp
halt as I am
and plod
this local hill
a pilgrim not my own
my stride lost
when I was found
my pace now seen
if it can be
in still small steps
my master makes in me

labor done

"...the seed sprouts and grows, though he does not know how"

[Mark 4:27]

labor done
kernels broadcast
I dream of increase
mind furrowed
I remember tender shoots

breathing slowly
deeply
I rest
knowing I am no root
no cause

though I've cast
no scattered seed
can look to me in hope
so in sleep
steeped in weakness
I dream of purpose and power

until with first light
fully risen
I see my field teeming
all my adding multiplied
seedlings of my labor's casting
stirring in the scythe-sharp wind
of the Lord who labors night and day
who is giving even now in me the growth
of his outcast life

at an age

at an age
when death has gotten in my face
and I know it will remain staring
with disarming openness
with a counterfeit of calm
and not from a distance
one eyebrow a little up
so as to say
so
what do you think?
still believe?
faced with the end of your age
do you think again?
was faith a hobby taken up
in your age of innocence?

well
first off
(not that I would talk to death)
these dying words were young once
young life said the same
said these age old things
from just as close
yes
before death was
life was up in my mid-morning face
selling easy ways and open options
recommending fame
saying
so
(breath sweetly in my face)
so
isn't faith for the desperate stage?
for terminal fear time?
a prop for the last age?
(you know:
dark creeps in
we begin to whistle)
what's to be, will
so why?
why hold your wrists
out front like that?
why be led away?
hmmm?
have your day

well
as for innocence
I never was that I recall
not at any age
not in ages of others either
not one innocent past
no not one
not even early pillars
(faced with questions too
breathed close in)

so
what do I think?
did they still believe?
do I?

well
yes
yes they did
yes I do
yes in every season

at any age
is not our unbelieving no
the desperate wheeze
of a shallow breather?
is not faith's way
wholly other?
believing's not for the faint
not for one whose heart
is in retreat
not for one who seeks an out

faith engages hand to hand
in a front line trench
after grace and bread
after soaking silence
faith goes out to find
gets right up in the mug of life
nose to nose with end-times too
eyes lit
both brows just a little up
so as to say

yes
I'm bound both hands
but led up into life
yes
I'm fixed both feet
but free to step in harvest fields

so
I'll have no strut-in-the-darkness life
I've surrendered mine
no door-to-nothing death
mine is swallowed up

yes
sometimes I wonder
am filled sometimes with wonder
at the last rejoining word:
Life who finds and frees
whose breath and word
come face to face
and heart to heart
from age to age
close in
and I begin again